Trespassing My Ancestral Lands

poems by

Kalpna Singh-Chitnis

Finishing Line Press
Georgetown, Kentucky

Trespassing My Ancestral Lands

Poetry

Copyright © 2024 by Kalpna Singh-Chitnis
ISBN 979-8-88838-568-5 First Edition
All rights reserved under International and Pan-American Copyright Conventions. No part of this book may be reproduced in any manner whatsoever without written permission from the publisher, except in the case of brief quotations embodied in critical articles and reviews.

ACKNOWLEDGMENTS

Poems Previously Published

The poems from *Trespassing My Ancestral Lands* have appeared in various literary publications, including *World Literature Today, Tupelo Quarterly, Cold Mountain Review, California Quarterly, Silk Routes Project* (IWP) at The University of Iowa, Stanford University's *Life in Quarantine, Pirene's Fountain, Pratik, Fine Lines, The Kali Project, Oxygen: Parables of the Pandemic, Sunflowers: Ukrainian Poetry on War Resistance Hope and Peace, Soul Spaces, The Mountain was Abuzz, Love isn't Audacity, Words and Worlds, Das Literarische, The Agonist, IHRAF Writes, Life and Legends, Muse India, SpillWords*, and in translations in various international journals.

Publisher: Leah Huete de Maines
Editor: Christen Kincaid
Cover Art: © Silent River
Cover Photos: © Dieter G.
Author Photos: Raymond Denton and Silent River
Copy Editing: Candice Louisa Daquin, Melissa Studdard and Kalpna Singh-Chitnis

Order online: www.finishinglinepress.com
also available on amazon.com

Author inquiries and mail orders:
Finishing Line Press
PO Box 1626
Georgetown, Kentucky 40324
USA

Contents

Foreword by Candice Louisa Daquin xiii

Trespassing My Ancestral Lands

History 1
Do You Know? 2
The Pending Introduction of KSC.. 3
The Language We Speak 4
America Held My Hand 5
Trespassing My Ancestral Lands 6
The Indus 8
The Abode of Gods 9
Three Leaves 11
Lala My Rikshawala 12
On My Way to School 13
Jacaranda 14
The Land of My Birth: The Light of Asia 15
Mirror 17
The Salt of a Woman 18
Sermon 19
What Becomes of a Ravished Woman? 20
Lipstick 21
Inferno 22
Scars 23
God's Take 24
The Sanity We Were Born With 25
Fatwa Against a Woman Who Renounces Her Veil 26
Revolution 27
A Desire of 'Self' Execution 28
Calling the Buddhas of Bamyan 29
The Daughters of the Hindu Kush 31
The Great Departure 33
Inheritance isn't a Matter of Choice 34
The Wisdom of My Ancestors 35
Birds are Our Ancestors 36
The Caged Bird 37
The Bridge 38
When Everything Becomes a Calling 39
Let the Water Sit all Night 40
Tripitaka 41

Dhaknesar 42
Roots 43
Another Shore 44
America 45
Invocation 46

Blood and Water

Simply a Witness 51
The Last Soldier 52
Sunflower 53
Ground Zero 54
War: A One Way Street 55
War and Flowers 56
My Post Office Without a Country 57
Love that Cannot Live Long Enough 58
Language 59
The Temples of Knowledge 60
The Peacebroker 62
The Best Kept Secret 63
Alan Kurdi 64
Jamila of Idlib 65
Line of Control 66
Dreamers 67
Displaced 68
The Painted Ladies of Baja 69

The Dance of the Century

At the Sound of Tsuzumi 73
O Captain! 74
Is Anyone Listening? 76
The Poet is Gone 78
Pandemic 79
ER 80

For My Ancestors

Impressions

Trespassing My Ancestral Lands captures the poet's eye roving the landscapes to see and discover the many layers of self in a multi-layered world of family, nature, and cycles of life. Kalpna Singh-Chitnis' voice is a hypnotic opera of cautionary tales. These heart-wrenching poems burn and sing to understand the primordial codes and rituals we depend on to give our lives meaning. An astute observer of the smallest details, she grips us with the travails of having feet firmly planted on both sides of the worlds and cultures. This brave poet walks the precipice and captures the testimonials of human grief, the dangers of love, loss, and war. Singh-Chitnis creates a voluminous experience of color and imagery rendering the mystical traditions and the hope in chaos. Kalpna Singh-Chitnis blows the shofar and shows how the power of language and story can lift us from despair, to reclaim our passions and our ghosts, the only way poetry can. This collection is indelible, you will come back again and again to a Motherland of wisdom—a talisman and guide to living with the fullest of fire and breath.
~**Cynthia Atkins,** author of *Still-Life with God*

Reader, if what you seek is an illusion, phantoms and figments of imagination written in fleeting, figurative language, then move on. Seeker, if what you wish to read is real, fleshed-out through direct, honorable verses which linger without pretentiousness, then don't pass by this book. "If you are a woman," Ms. Singh-Chitnis sings, "tell my story to your sons. If you are a man, tell it to your daughters. If you are a preacher, teach it as a sermon to the believers." Here is a Human Being speaking equally to all other Human Beings, one who "trespasses," too, across limitations of gender, ethnicity, nationality; whose story thus becomes a story worth telling, and retelling, and retelling again. For in the poem, "The Salt of a Woman," as she writes so sublimely, "Her story is much older than her civilization…" The story found in *Trespassing My Ancestral Lands*, is in fact as old as Creation itself.
~**Jennifer Reeser,** author of *Indigenous* and *Strong Feather*

I would like to stand on street corners asking people to read *Trespassing My Ancestral Lands*. The enduring necessity of this collection of poetry far exceeds the ordinary every day and as such, I would wish it to be widely shared. Very infrequently, in my role as editor, I come across a collection that blows me away. Figuratively, literally, and spiritually. Singh-Chitnis is a deeply modern writer, who dips her pen in ancient history and acknowledgment of what came before us. She blends these disparate worlds together in such a way we learn and grow with each insight. This is the sheer essence of a poet, to be both translator and third-eye for the reader. When we are unable to articulate our feelings, the poet can. Singh-Chitnis has an uncanny canary-in-a-coal-mine prescience that feels at times like she's reading our minds. If a poet cannot speak for her readers, she's stuck in a confessional style that grows dusty with time. To stay alive long after her physical form has passed, she must transcend time and space and be the mouthpiece for our deepest fears and joys. I would go as far as saying if you don't like poetry, you might well be converted by this poetry because it's poetry, and it's more than poetry. She will be a poet we talk about in two hundred years. Her name won't simply be synonymous with good writing, it will be a legacy.
~**Candice Louisa Daquin,** Senior Editor / Indie Blu(e) Publishing and author of *Tainted by the Same Counterfeit* among others

Kalpna Singh-Chitnis is not looking for bystanders or onlookers to her powerful poems of personal journey. What she is looking for is a companion and to that end she uses her skill as a poet to draw the reader ever closer, so close at times that we hear her heart beating within these compelling narrative poems. Her fine writing holds a clarity that shows both how some distances can bring us near and how only words sometimes keep us apart. I think any reader that joins Kalpna Singh-Chitnis on her journey of memory and self-reflection will find themselves inwardly rewarded without measure.
	~**Beau Beausoleil,** author of *Concealed in Language* and *Another Way Home*

An unforgettable poetry collection for the soul it seeks and lays bare, and one that embraces and urges the reader to rise and perceive life in distinctive and myriad ways. As a true poet, Kalpna Singh-Chitnis finds poetry in everything, particularly in vocalizing immigrant experiences, loss of native identity, and the duality of the diasporic scaffold. She further fuses these vividly within the framework of the past, present, and future, thereby creating breathtaking edifices of life and memorializing our existence. Nostradamus-like, her poetry in turn signals our future as well. Singh-Chitnis's historical, cultural, confessional, and observational views and words leave us probing, enriched, and satiated."
	~**Anita Nahal,** writer, and professor; author of drenched thoughts (novel) and poetry collections, "*Kisses at the espresso bar*" and *What's wrong with us Kali women?* among others

Kalpna Singh-Chitnis writes poems with quiet urgency, poems highlighting and condemning violence and social persecution perpetrated against women, against immigrants, against anyone who has lost a homeland. But don't expect rhetoric and abstraction here; rather, find intimate poems addressed to all of us, like letters hand-written with the language of loss: "What have I lost to deserve the beauty around me," Singh-Chitnis asks, and there is no answer outright, but glimpses of one whose broken wings will stretch for a lifetime.
	~**Octavio Quintanilla**, author of the poetry collection, *If I Go Missing* (Slough Press) and *The Book of Wounded Sparrows* (Texas Review Press)

Foreword: Trespassing My Ancestral Lands

A foreword cannot proffer the heart of another's work and convince the reader of its innate worth. If it could, I would request this introduction did just that. I would like to stand on street corners asking people to read *Trespassing My Ancestral Lands*, by Kalpna Singh-Chitnis. The enduring necessity of this collection of poetry far exceeds the ordinary everyday and as such, I would wish it to be widely shared.

Very infrequently, in my role as editor, I come across a collection that blows me away. Figuratively, literally and spiritually. Perhaps as editors, we work through many mediocre and 'good' collections, hoping for that one diamond in the rough. Perhaps it is only one book in a lifetime. After all, if you were to ask yourself how many books have stayed with you, ten, twenty years hence. What would you say? Simply put, there are not many pure sublime, incredible, irreplaceable books. They simply don't exist.

Fear runs through my body.
The pain of the woman being flogged is familiar to my skin. (The Daughters of the Hindu Kush).

For a reader of literature and poetry, this may seem at odds with our wide appreciation for literature and poetry, but in truth, writing a book that can impress on a fundamental level, is rare. Having read *The Tree* and other poetry by Kalpna Singh-Chitnis and knowing her prodigious output and reputation for excellence, I wasn't surprised her work was exemplary, but it surprised me nonetheless. That is what *once-in-a-lifetime* books do for the reader, they captivate you. They enthrall and create lasting wonderment.

there are no kings and queens in Kashmir anymore.
They all died in a Raid long ago, and
their subjects have been defeated in the game of
Check and Mate, we all have played along together. (Invocation).

The real question is why? What sets Singh-Chitnis apart from the rest? I know many fine poets, and I read poetry books every single day as part of my job. Singh-Chitnis writes in a way that has gravitas but also, immediacy and tender familiarity. There is a haunting intensity to her work that I have not found elsewhere. As I read her work, I find myself simultaneously envious of her brilliance and stunned into appreciative silence. She speaks for generations; she is not only a poet but a soothsayer of truth and insight. It's about *how* she says what she says, as much as *what* she says.

They traveled to the borders to welcome refugees
and sat on shrines to pray for peace.
And before they wilted in fire and snow,
the flowers scattered their seeds to regrow.
Everyone takes a new role in a war. (War and Flowers).

We talk of wordsmiths, we bandy around ideas of talent and alacrity without really considering, what creates magic? With the best intentions in the world, a writer can market themselves, go to poetry readings, promote their work and network, but they may never be more than *'good'* which is still an achievement. To be more than that, to be unparalleled, shockingly talented, perhaps unsurpassable, well that is surely not something we can learn. It is simply our natural state. Few people possess that tongue, that verbiage, and try as they might, no MFA program can teach it. You either have it or you do not.

The idea of who we are is not limited to our narrow discretion.
I'm a person, and a nation, an ally, and an adversary. (War: A One Way Street).

Reading Kalpna Singh-Chitnis' work reminds me of watching live dance. You go into a theatre, the lights are lowered, everyone is silent. The music begins. You are carried away with the swell and anticipation, it feels almost erotic in its intensity. Then the dancers move and their seemingly effortless fluidity and matching tempo to the music, entrance you. As you leave the theatre, you turn to your companions and try to put into words how you felt. Invariably you never can. That kind of feeling is impossible to describe and perhaps of the moment. It stays with you like a cherished memory even as it's not as intimate as it feels. You are forever changed by it.

I had returned, only to inherit her fears,
and the fear of having everything she never had
and knowing—there is no death for a life never lived. (Roots).

Kalpna Singh-Chitnis is a dancer of words. Her nimble, seemingly effortless ability with a language that is not her first, wrecks notions of fluency. She reaches heights in her understanding of how to convey the impossible. It feels downright spiritual. As much as I may support and value other poets, when I read a poem by Singh-Chitnis we're simply entering another league. She is the youthful *grande dame* of poetry, not just poetry by Indian poets writing in English, but any poet, in any language.

The mind is nothing but tainted water in the body of clay,
spun on the wheel of the unknown.
Be still and breathe like earthenware and cool off. (Let the Water Sit All Night).

I can no longer touch my Oud or weave a dream whirling the cosmos.
But the valley of Bamyan remains silent. Its cliffs stare blankly (Calling the Buddhas of Bamyan).

If I did not know Kalpna Singh-Chitnis' legacy thus far, and were unaware of her multitude of achievements, I can say, hand on heart, my response to this collection would be exactly the same. It is not contingent upon my awareness of her existing talent as a filmmaker, an actor on life's stage, a publisher, writer and philosopher. Without knowing anything more than the book in my hands, I would open *Trespassing my Ancestral Lands* and weep. Not just in sorrow, but in joy, in realization and with that shuddering emotion rarely found in the modern world.

We inherit the dreams aborted from
the eyes of our forefathers and mothers. (Inheritance isn't a Matter of Choice).

Kalpna Singh-Chitnis writes simply. But this doesn't mean she writes without finesse or depth. It means she knows how to nail a point without belaboring it. She recognizes instinctively how to reach into your understanding directly and to illuminate those necessary observations and insights, in such a way few know how to do. I could quote her forever, she has that immediacy, and sophistication of thought that appears simply put but few get right. Surely this alone marks her as a poet of unparalleled brilliance and staying power.

The only thing I know is that I come and go.
Someday, I'll rise beyond the horizon
to tell this story to my children, continuing my journey. (The Wisdom of My Ancestors).

It is equally rare to read through an entire collection and not find some extraneous work that is weaker and perhaps filler for the rest. *Trespassing My Ancestral Lands* has no weaker poems, no *'I'd better fill in the gaps'* kind of work that reduces the overall high consistency of writing. Every single poem has measurable power and testimonial worth. This is why I am an advocate for shorter collections with poetry. Few can stand large tomes and if we think of some of the best poetry books historically, they are often precise, grafted and succinctly intentional. Less is more.

I'm not here to decide
whether a war is just or unjust.
I'm Time; simply a witness. (Simply a Witness)

I have never quoted an entire poem in a review, because it is important to leave a lot back, so the reader can experience the pleasure of unrevealed work for the first time. However, to illustrate my point, consider this poem in its entirety:

He asked for my introduction.
I wrote it in a hundred words.
He didn't like it.

He altered my bio.

I refused to accept.
He took me down.
That's how our history was written. (History).

This short poem opens *Trespassing My Ancestral Lands*. At once it embodies Singh-Chitnis' unique style. She is able to say so much in a few words, she's also able to speak in layers. Her work doesn't fall into the category of 'sharable meme' because it's more intelligent than that. But like a Haiku Master, she can transliterate truth without needing multiple stanzas. You can interpret this poem as what it appears to be on the surface, a poem about submitting work to publishers, and the result. But there's always more. How much more depends upon how long you sit with these words. I read them as a universal message about how we fight for ourselves. We have a biography within each of us, few accept, many try to obliterate. To keep ourselves alive, we must refuse to be reduced. As a woman. As an Indian woman. As a woman over a certain age. As a beautiful woman. As a writer. As a human being. The varied ways we refuse to be edited out, speak to our fortitude and lasting determination. This also is the essence of Kalpna Singh-Chitnis. Hence why it's such a perfect opening poem for this collection.

Imagine if you will, the journey of her life. Intensely spiritual, her Buddhist soul searching for greater understanding and release, as her physical self must live in the modern world, at times jarring and unsettling for those in touch with the natural and spiritual. Now we can begin to understand that *Trespassing My Ancestral Lands* isn't simply about a woman of color, an immigrant, an Indian, a woman in a man's world, a mother, a successful business woman. This is about her personal spiritual walk. Her *claim*. Her soul. How many poetry books reveal a woman's soul? How many can touch us with that kind of wicked-clever, piercing insight?

A Painted Lady in my backyard—poses for a picture,
and asks me—Where have You come from? (The Painted Ladies of Baja)

How often do we learn alongside the 'devil being in the details'—and come to an understanding of the way others live, how they are brought up and how that experience is indelible, and valuable. Too often we dismiss anything outside the soundbite or the *trend*, and it is the enduring value of books to remind us and teach us, what we forget and do not yet know. You don't become enlightened reading Facebook. You become enlightened when you stop, empty yourself and listen. Reading is a form of listening. Breathe in the experiences of others, and know more of the whole.

"Close your eyes to see all you cannot see with your eyes open," (The Temples of Knowledge).

Singh-Chitnis is a deeply modern writer, who dips her pen in ancient history and acknowledgement of what came before us. She blends these disparate worlds together in such a way we learn and grow with each insight. This is the sheer essence of a poet, to be both translator and third-eye for the reader. When we are unable to articulate our feelings, the poet can. Singh-Chitnis has an uncanny *canary-in-a-coal-mine* prescience that feels at times like she's reading our minds. If a poet cannot speak for her readers, she's stuck in a confessional style that grows dusty with time. To stay alive long after her physical form has passed, she must transcend time-and-space and be the mouth piece for our deepest fears and joys.

They are considering a mental asylum or a senior home.
They are waiting for her lab results and the doctor's note.
She no longer has a say. (Is Anyone Listening?)

Even the title of this collection is multi-layered. Think of what it means to trespass your own ancestry? Consider what land means, beyond the literal? And how we reclaim ourselves when we are both apart and still present? As an immigrant, I deeply appreciated how Singh-Chitnis nails the diaspora dislocation many immigrants feel, and simultaneously owns the loss whilst thriving in her transplanted country. This brings hopefulness as well as a visceral depiction of the reality of immigration, poverty, suffering and all that it entails.

Why do I worry? Thirty-three million gods will take care of everything.
Why do I bother? 1.36 billion people will manage their country.
O sister, you will be okay. O Mother, try to sleep now. (O Captain!).

If you are an immigrant, you can well appreciate the uprooting this involves, even how the water tastes different. The subtle ways you don't fit in and have to find your feet again. *Trespassing My Ancestral Lands* is as much about that journey as it is this woman's life, her loves, her passions, her secrets, the pain and joy of her life. At times it is disquieting just how capably she achieves this. But having been editor of several poetry anthologies herself, who is more qualified to speak to this intentionality? And with a humility rather than a brash confidence. In *The Pending Introduction of KSC*, I felt myself transported into a vignette of inequality and racism that infuriated me and yet, its depiction burns through me so intensely, it reminds me why poetry achieves this like no other art-form can.

Everyone comes and goes,
I do not leave. I must keep waiting until
someone introduces me. (The Pending Introduction of KSC)

Writers who try to be too clever, miss that subtlety whilst Singh-Chitnis writes simply but each poem contains mosaics upon mosaics of deeper meaning. She achieves this time-and-again without pretension or self-consciousness. Unlike some male writers before her, she doesn't insist on knowing everything, quite the opposite. Her translation of being female is frank, physical and compassionate, needing no ego. It is as if we are diving into a deep pool of her mind. I would go as far as saying, if you don't like poetry, you might well be converted by this poetry, because it's poetry and its more than poetry. It's truth. In her poem *The Language We Speak*, there is such an evocation of what it means to exist, I can't think of anyone who can describe this better:

And one day, I emptied all the letters of my tongue
into a chest, locked them, and went silent.
I did not starve, but I felt deprived.
I wasn't abandoned, but I felt alone. (The Language We Speak)

I am not Indian. But the pleasure of working with writers from India has opened a veritable universe for me, that I never wish to leave. I can't pretend to fully appreciate all of the specific cultural references as much as I want to, but Singh-Chitnis helps me want to learn and grow. I can appreciate ancestry, the pains of being discriminated against, the loss of my land, and culture, and the raw way Singh-Chitnis presents this in her writing is unmatched and deeply moving:

I'm bewildered in the desert like a Darwīsh,
like a Sufi, leaving behind a trail of songs
for a caravan lost in the desert storms. (Trespassing My Ancestral Lands).

The last poem in the collection haunted me. Kalpna Singh-Chitnis has an uncanny ability to know *where* poems should be placed. She doesn't make mistakes in her arrangement, she's like a pianist who hits the right notes without thinking about them. A composer of the world's orchestra. Her instinctual arrangement has a language of its own. I understood why she put *ER* as the last poem. It may seem disparate but it speaks to everything else:

I just had some internal injuries no one knew.
I bled inside. I died in front of everyone,
without anyone noticing me. (ER)

This isn't about attention-seeking or notoriety. This is about a woman's heart. What she has silently endured, is her walk. It is at times unbearably honest and I find myself reading with open mouth and wet eyes. There is a universe here: Humor. Grief. Loss. Gain. Love. If you don't know what life is about, you will know more after reading *Trespassing My Ancestral Lands*. To write for us all, takes a writer who transcends the ordinary and is able to fearlessly speak. Historically there's been much latitude for men to accomplish this, but less for women, less still for women from India. I am thrilled to read this woman's work and know she is part of that essential movement. *Is anyone listening?* I hope so.

As I said, I expected an excellent book. But even with this expectation, I was surprised at how much I fell in love with this collection. As a writer, I can say without self-deprecation, I couldn't write this. I wish I could but I don't have it in me. I so admire Kalpna Singh-Chitnis on a professional level, watching her hone her craft in ways few ever achieve. I am proud of her, and in awe of that recipe for brilliance she possesses. Few of us can ever hope to put something like this together, and I suspect she's going to do it again and again. She will be a poet we talk about in 200 years. Her name won't simply be synonymous with good writing, it will be a legacy.

Candice Louisa Daquin

Senior Editor / Indie Blu(e) Publishing
Consultant Editor / Raw Earth Ink / BlackBird Press
Poetry Editor / Parcham / The Pine Cone Review

Trespassing My Ancestral Lands

History

He asked for my introduction.
I wrote it in a hundred words.
He didn't like it.

He altered my bio.

I refused to accept.
He took me down.
That's how our history was written.

Do You Know

Do you know what it means
to be uprooted from your soil?

Ask a tree.

You will never see the same sky again.
You will never drink from the same well.
You will never again taste the earth
that gave you birth.

Do you know what it means for a tree
to be rooted again in a sanctuary?

Ask me.

The Pending Introduction of KSC

I'm not sure if it's pitiful or powerful
but here I am, trying to make sense of everything.

I do not know why Timothy Jones, sitting next to me
in our class, chose not to make my introduction
when we all introduced a student sitting next to us.

Mr. Meisner went blank when he asked him,
if he could introduce Allen instead.

Was it because I was a woman?
Was it because I was colored?
Was it because I was different?

I do not know why Mr. Meisner
didn't question Timothy Jones.

I do not know why I didn't question
Mr. Meisner myself.
I just sat there like a stump of a tree.

I am still sitting there in my class,
for the past twenty-five years,
next to Timothy Jones,

waiting for Mr. Meisner to come
and ask him that question.
But will he ever return?

The lectures begin and end,
but the questions remain.
Everyone comes and goes,

but I do not leave.
I must keep waiting until
someone introduces me.

The Language We Speak

How could you have possibly heard me?
I barely knew your language before so,
let my heart fade with one last remorse
should you ever want to know,

why I traveled so far from the land
to which I belonged and did not belong.
I could not speak sooner, I know, I know...
My words were inadequate, lumped in my throat.

And one day, I emptied all the letters of my tongue
into a chest, locked them, and went silent.
I did not starve, but I felt deprived.
I wasn't abandoned, but I felt alone.

I wasn't lost, but I couldn't find
what I was looking for, and one day,
I died. I was buried in your bosom
like a Pharaoh…

with all my grains and gold,
with all my silk and songs,
with all my love and loss,
and now, I am one with you.

I am your mountains and prairies.
I am your oceans and deserts.
I am your air and sunshine.
O America!

I am your glory and prayers.
I am your shame and guilt.
I am your pride and prejudice.
I am the language we speak.

America Held My Hand

Once exited from our mother's womb,
is it possible to return to it?

Once departed from our homeland
is it possible to go back again?

Everyone remained silent,
coping with the answers,

America held my hand.

Trespassing My Ancestral Lands

In my dreams, I often trespass
my ancestral lands,

looking for the centuries hidden in the hills,
finding history lost in the sands,

searching for an oracle safe in ruins,
not to be found and read.

I often venture without any food and water
in the land of five rivers,

emerging through the passages of
a glorious civilization.

I have no shoes, only my garb and a scarf,
that I'm afraid of losing to the desert winds.

An amulet strung around my neck reads
an *Aayat* of the Quran.

May Almighty bless the daughter of the idol worshipers
out to defy borders and demarcations,

there were only destinations
before the birth of nations.

In my dreams, I often wonder,
who carved my face and disappeared in the winds.

I wonder,
where my ancestors came from.

 Were they natives; Aryan, Mughal, Turk,
Greek, Mongol, or Tughluq?

What mountains did they cross?
What oceans did they brave?

And the roads they traveled,
were they made of silk, rocks, or gravel?

What battles did they fight,
before surrendering to light?

Where did they sleep, away from their homes?
In *Ordo*, palaces, or *Viharas*?

What food did they eat?
What songs did they write and sing?

Did they speak Sanskrit, Prakrit,
Khadi, Farsi, or Pashto?

I'm bewildered in the desert like a Darwīsh,
like a Sufi, leaving behind a trail of songs

for a caravan lost
in the desert storms.

In my dreams, I search for the Buddha in a forest,
Muhammad in a cave, and Jesus in Jerusalem,

I look for Krishna on a battlefield and
Chanakya in Takṣaśilā,

In the alleys of towns and villages,
I look for Ghalib, Rumi, and Khayyám,

In the temples, I look for Meera, Kabir,
Tulsi, and Rama in a *Gurukul*.

In my dreams, I remain uncaptured.
In my dreams, my dreams are valid.

In my dreams, I sleep
in the seven continents,

and wake up with the sun
rising on the roof of the universe.

An eagle hovers over me in the skies,
flapping wings, shedding colors, protecting my dreams,

that can never be a part of history—
you will ever like to write.

The Indus

With the first ray of the primordial dawn,
she arose from her slumber deep,
sowing the seeds of life, inviting the world,
to come to the feast to her land of splendor.

Her harvest, a spectacle, was a cosmic delight.
She winnowed the chaffs and crushed the grains
upon metamorphic rocks, kneaded dough—
within the basin crusts of her glistening rivers.

She baked the bread fragrant, upon the fire of
erupting volcanoes, served her children meals
on the tectonic plates of the drifting continents
and went into labor, marching in the mud,

birthing the civilization of Sindh, that you called it
Indus and Hind, Harappa and Mohenjo-Daro,
Dholavira and Rakhigarhi,
Mehrgarh and Ganweriwala.

She thrust the mighty Himalayas to the height of the sky,
tinted her forests green, painted flowers and fruits on the scene.
She sculpted oceans, carved the reservoirs of sweet water
and set free her rivers, serene.

She spread her tresses, glistening with gold,
and created the desert of Thar. She dried the linens of eras
wet and cold on the linings of her memories,
unfurled divine clouds across the azure skies.

She carried silk, spices and salt from her shores
on her voyages to distant lands and returned home with
shells, pearls, cotton and horses. She beckoned gods
from celestial realms to bless her fertile lands.

And her valleys echoed with the sacred hymns of the Vedas,
chanted by saints, seers and sages, upon her holy riverbanks.
No earthly laws ruled her domain. Her children followed
nature's course, and worshiped the divine in all that existed.

She forged her nation with glory and pride, and called it Bharat.
She was a goddess and a mother, a queen and a protector.
The one you call Indus and Hind is beloved Sindh, the genesis of
a glorious civilization, resilient and prosperous, luminous and sacred.

The Abode of Gods

(A Tribute to Himalaya)

How long have you been there, sitting like a sage,
watching time come and go from your peaks
bathed in gold with the sunrise and sheathed in the silver of
the moon and stars, sewn into the canopy of the night sky,
inscribing profound realizations on the sheets of water and clouds?

When I think of our forebears, I see your reflection in them.
I discover their footprints on your trails, preserved in snow,
their delightful presence still somewhere in your prosperous valleys,
their homes—filled with the scent of your rare flowers and shrubs,
their kitchens stocked with your herbs, fruits, seeds, saffron, and salt.

You are ancient among all yogis and sages
from the time of Shiva and Kashyapa.
You're among the earliest known *Bodhisattvas*,
from the time of the countless lineages of *Tathagatas*.
O the abode of Padmasambhava and Prashara,

You are the first among all warriors, defending—
the peripheries of your motherland and continent.
Our ancestors inherited your strength and solidity.
You gifted them your wisdom, grace, and glory.
I hear the murmurs of your mighty rivers in their veins,

their minds bearing the serenity of your placid lakes,
every atom of their existence echoing your legends,
and their unending quests of seeking themselves.
When I think of our ascendants, I see you arise in them
and realize, I'm more than my eyes could ever see.

I'm as young as a new leaf on a tree that grows from
your ancient heart, and as old as the time of your conception and birth.
O Himalaya, I see the reflections of your summit,
in the waters of your lakes, warm and afloat in my eyes,
and your swans swimming in its tranquility.

Yet my mind is often gripped by the agitation of
the winds and storms you have always weathered
with philosophical calm. Your strength sustains me.
In the palms of my hands, I see—
your mountains rising, your rivers meandering,

your clouds crossing over the continents, and
your air traveling to me through invisible channels.
When I breathe, I inhale the eras bygone.
When I exhale, I see the miracles unfold in the present.
I see a newly born fawn, opening its curious eyes in your lap,

fledglings learning to fly, serpents sloughing off their skin,
flowers discovering their beauty in the mirrors of
your waters and sky. I see fruits being born on trees
and bees describing the sweetness of honey to the forests.
In your foothills, mountain tribes are singing harvest songs.

At sundown, they are baking bread for their children;
their faces are lit like topaz in the glow of embers. They sing
with their coral lips, and smile with their green, sapphire eyes.
They drink the nectar of your sweetest fruits
and dance around the fire under a snowy moon.

With the sound of gongs and dungchen rising from Gompas,
Buddhas are awakening in your caverns. They will protect
your glaciers, and diminish the sufferings of the universe.
With the sounds of cymbals and hymn chants rising from
your serene river banks, I see time marching ahead—

beyond the concepts of time, with the flow of your
bubbling brooks; with the flights of your birds;
following the dial of the sun; the paths of the planets
toward a destination found at every step,
and the *Devas* in their abode, delight!

Three Leaves

My childhood home opens into a palm grove
laden with the far-reaching fruits of Palmyras.
Beyond the rows of palms are fields
where farmers sow their dreams.

The eastern sky halves like a palm fruit, dark-purple,
with an orange spell, secreting white sap. And the sun
appears like a yellow dot of sandalwood paste—
Grandma grinds on a stone slab to write *"Om,"*
the primordial sound encoded in a word, painted on
the sacred leaves of the Wood Apple, the *Bael Patras*.

Three leaves on a stem to offer Shiva,
the three-eyed Yogi, glancing at the universe from
the left, right, and center. The three leaves
for the three phases of time, the past, present, and future.
The three leaves, for the three forces of nature—
creation, preservation, annihilation.

Grandma never explained the rituals to me.
My ancestors did not offer wisdom to anyone without asking.
Knowledge is a thing to be discovered.
One must know the difference between knowing and learning,
the secret to knowing oneself.

Lala My Rikshawala

Hurry, hurry!
Lala, my *Rikshawala* hollers.

He takes me to school.
Barefoot in winter, he pedals fast,
but the wheel of time has its own pace.

I tuck my icy hands under my arms.
The blue cardigan knit by my mother keeps me warm.
I have books to read and lunch in a tiffin box.

I'm privileged. Lala isn't.
He knows why. I don't.

On My Way to School

On my way to school is a *Desi* bar. I often see
drunken men ejected from there, with loose women.

One stole my uncle. My aunt spits in her face.
She had a love child, disgraced.

On my way to school, people stand in a queue to fill water
supplied from a municipal tap before it shuts off at nine.

On my way to school is a Banyan tree. It yawns in the morning.
Monkeys and bears dance on the street, and cows chew cud.

On my way to school are shops selling *Samosa, Jalebi,
Pakoda*, and Tea. Beggars sit there all day, hoping for a piece.

On my way to school is a grain mill, by the hill, and a market.
Fresh produce arrives there every morning from local farms.

On my way to school are butcher shops.
Animals are skinned in the open.

Chickens crammed into cages, and goats tethered by ropes
shudder in fear, waiting for their turn.

On my way to school are temples, Gurdwaras and mosques,
and prayers blaring from loudspeakers for the ever-silent gods.

On my way to school are potholes and standing water.
Dogs and Cobblers sit under shades, and my father buys cigarettes.

On my way to school is a railway crossing.
People often go there to end their life.

On my way to school, what I learn,
isn't taught to us in school.

Jacaranda

Jacaranda blooming in my backyard
brings me the hope of Spring's purple-blue.

Its elegant rows on the streets of California
remind me of *Gulmohar,* the Flamboyant trees
ablaze in Spring and Summer in my country afar.

I ate lunch at my school
under the scant shade of a *Gulmohar,*
admiring its orange-red flowers.

I wonder if the tree still stands
in my school's playground
and carries now, my memories.

I list every tree I remember seeing
while growing up, and hope,
they remember me too,

a child wanting to attain their fruits,
a girl swinging from their branches.
O my swings! The ropes...!

Marks appear on my hand.
The haze of purple-blue
 stretches over the continents revolving.

What have I lost to deserve the beauty around me?

The Land of My Birth: The Light of Asia

   —*For Gaya and Bodhgaya*

I carry my city in the marrow of my bones.
In my flesh, its ancient roads swell up in monsoon.

I go around, carrying my town in every cell of my body,
its bare mountains resting on my shoulders, its cursed river
running through my veins, its history in the layers of my skin.

Every memory of my city is an affirmation.
I carry them safe in the pockets of my heart, like receipts,
their ink still fresh, their promises still valid.

Much water has flown under the sand of the Falgu, the Niranjana,
which still reminisces the eras of the Vedas and Puranas,
the exile of Rama, Laxman, and Sita, the final rites of Dashrath,

the liberation of souls taking place on her banks,
on a Vesak full moon, under the Pipal tree, Sujata offering
rice pudding to a mendicant, soon to be the Buddha,

and the winds chanting hymns; singing
the songs of Sufi, Ata Hussain Fani.
The ground of my town still safeguards,

the footprints of Vishnu, *Tirthankaras*, and lost emperors.
Its mountains still ponder the sermons of the Buddha—
"*Bhikkus,* everything is burning."

"*And what is all that is burning?*"
"*The eye is burning, forms are burning,*
eye-consciousness is burning, eye contact is burning..."

"*Burning with what?*"
"*Burning with the fire of lust, hate, and delusion.*
Burning with birth, aging, death, sorrows and lamentations..."*

O, the city of light, the land of Nirvana,
the land of my ancestors and Vihars,
the seat of my soul and precious birth,

I'm made of your dust.
You are me. I'm you!

*Adittapariyaya Sutta: Adittapariyaya Sutta, known as "The Fire Sermon," was delivered by the Buddha on Gayasisa Parvat, alternatively called Brahmayoni Hill, located in Gaya, the author's hometown, in the state of Bihar, India. The Sutta has been translated from Pali by Ñanamoli Thera, with an alternate translation provided by Thanissaro Bhikku.

Mirror

They would call her Kali,
tease her with a Bollywood song—
"See the raven fly like a swan..."

Playing hopscotch in the street,
she would run at once, into her house.
She hated the song and the bully kids.

She would lock herself in a room
and look at her face in the mirror
a piercing gaze in her olive skin.

Her lips were lilac.
There was a fire glowing in her brown eyes
like the gold filament of violets.

She was beautiful. Mirrors don't lie.
She made all the mirrors of the world her friend.
But the story didn't end…

The Salt of a Woman

Here she goes down, again,
like a tree. Bark naked,
her flowers stolen, fruits eaten,
tongue clipped, and vagina axed.

From every stem of her body oozes
the salt of a woman, and her tears
like the ancient rivers of her land.

Her story is much older than her civilization
invaded and plundered, conquered and gifted,
questioned and blamed, dismissed and shamed,
over and over and over again.

Sermon

If I die of an assault,
do not file a report.
It isn't the first time.

Do not go to a court
seeking justice.
There is none.

Do not allow politicians to enter
my village and town.
No media, no clowns.

No debauchery of *whataboutery*.
Do not bother hanging my perpetrators,
they will be born again in a multitude.

Do not imprison them.
They can't be restrained.
I'll be violated again, just in another place and time.

If you hope to do anything for change,
write an epic or a tale in my name,
and teach it if you can, in every school on earth.

If you are a woman, tell my story to your sons.
If you are a man, tell it to your daughters.
If you are a preacher, teach it as a sermon to the believers.

What Becomes of a Ravished Woman?

A ravished woman turns into incense.
The ashes of her body are to fold in her fluids.
The splinters of her bones are sticks to roll on.

Her spirit ignites. In her flame—

She burns like Eucalyptus and Sandalwood,
Rose and Jasmine, Champa, Frankincense,
Tulsi and Sage.

Her perfume lingers heavily in the air.

Lipstick

Remember the day I had put on
lipstick for the first time?
Not red, not pink; a brown lipstick
suited to the color of my skin.

No one would have noticed,
but you did and thought
I had found love. Or at least,
I was looking for it.

You were worried that
the day I would find love,
it would stain your reputation.
You were told, love isn't found.

It is cultivated or negotiated.
You protested against me.
I wasn't as good as my sisters and cousins,
who never had the audacity to do *such a thing*.

Years later, you came to me and
looked for lipstick in my vanity case.
You preferred red. If not, a brighter shade of brown
will do. But I didn't carry lipstick anymore.

You insisted I buy one,
put it on, and go out to live a little.
But you didn't realize, Mother,
it was too late to find love.

Inferno

Nothing should have mattered;
his sadness, his grief,
his heart tossed in a dark river by an evil witch.

She should have known better.
There was no one else to blame.
The lover was slain by his own hatred,
and was left to die in a sinking boat.

His heart had surrendered to the darkness.
He was drowned in a bottle.
There was no one to rescue.
She should have known better, but she didn't.

Go to them, who will violate you, and rejoice it!
A woman patriarch?
A woman priest?
How dare!

A nightmare unfolds, and animals appear—
fearful, from the mountain trails,
to see the human feed on the human soul
in sheer astonishment.

Scars

You have bruises on your body, I said.

None of your business,
she responded and left.

I carry her scars now.

God's Take

God was a genius.
He had the reckoning. Thus,
when He created the universe,
He chose to be a man.

Then He defied himself and
evolved into everything
known and unknown,
to orchestrate the entire show.

You may not recognize
but those protesting before
the citadel of justice is Him.
But He can't be detained.

All prisons together cannot confine God.
He can't be forced to live in a woman's womb
if she isn't ready to bear God or his children.
God refuses to be an intruder.

You can't show him your calendar
and tell him it's too late!
He carries His own almanac.
Read His letters with caution!

You can't try Him in your courts.
He forges decrees of His own.
You can't go after Him. He will elude you.
He will escape from one state to another.

He has many places to go.
He will defy your verdict
and take away your gavel,
all the way to heaven.

The Sanity We Were Born With

The earth decides what grows in her womb.
When does God meddle in her right to choose?

Let's safeguard our youth struck in classrooms,
and citizens slain in the streets in a fleeting pulse.

They could have been us! Our right to defend ourselves
must not be at the cost of our right to live.

Let's breathe, and allow others to breathe as well.
Let's weep together if smiles bid farewell.

Let's cleanse our hands stained with blood of our own.
Let's summon our braves home from the fields of strife.

Let's bring to the refuge, those without hope,
suffering from hunger and illnesses.

Let's trade guns for roses to honor life.
Let's regain the sanity we were born with.

Fatwa Against a Woman Who Renounces Her Veil

At the moment, I'm totally in a mess,
searching frantically for some missing heartbeats.

Let's talk love right now. Who knows what's next?
Who knows, I'm shot by a cop in my face, as I speak,

or a rocket is launched on my land by a dictator, for not caving in fear,
or a *Fatwa* is issued against me for renouncing my veil?

I have outgrown my heavens and am not afraid of hell.
Let's talk love right now. Who knows what's next?

Revolution

I often grow restless by the noises outside.
I want to go out and march with you.
I want to shout, holding a banner, to bring a revolution.

I want to dismantle my myth and curse my enemies.
I want to demand justice.

Instead, I enter a house waiting for me in silence,
where my tongue becomes my eyes
and my eyes become my ears.

I surrender to my enemies there
and lie defenseless on the floor.

I can still hear the noises on the streets.
But I no longer feel the urge to speak.
I'm disenchanted by every slogan I wrote.

Ever since I have acquainted myself with my enemy,
I see a revolution within.

A Desire for 'Self' Execution

When the head feels like a gourd,
I want to scoop out all that it holds.

Everything I once considered important
must be re-examined now.

I want to take out every fiber of my brain,
and the seeds of all my ideas to carve emptiness.

I want to feel that hollowness, and smell the scent
released from the execution of my Self.

I want to sit at my door and welcome Autumn,
with a tealight candle flickering in me,

a little fire, enough to keep me warm,
yet insufficient to kill the frost gripping.

I want to watch ghosts and goblins pass me by, grinning at life,
and children excited for *trick or treat* in their colorful costumes.

I no longer care to fly like a witch with my broom,
or go door to door with my pail, knocking for candies.

I just want to sit out there at my doorstep like a pumpkin,
holding a lantern lit in me, and feel anything but important.

Calling the Buddhas of Bamyan

Bound for the city of sorrows, to the valley of screams,
I trespass the lands of my ancestors back in my dream.

I arrive at my citadel all alone. My clothes are torn.
The mirrors and beads of my *Kameez* are missing.

I'm no longer a princess decked out in ornaments.
The evening sky is a *Chador* I wrap around

and sleep on a mound of centuries, listening to the legends,
looking for a sign of hope in the northern sky.

I invite the sacred souls and winds from the eras gone by,
to recite the mantras of peace and healing that I can no longer hum.

What has become of the land, once the height of *Dharma* and glory?
I dream in an ancient language and speak to the Buddhas of Bamyan.

The white men have returned to the West with their shattered pride,
yet no peace has arrived in your land, tell me why?

The rocks, rivers, and soil of your nation lost
in the maze of time, are still red with

the blood of its people. Its children are
still standing at the crossroads.

I can hear the grieving of the young brides and widows behind veils.
Whose curse Kandahar carries like a cross on its shoulders?

Whose blessings still guard the mountains of the Hindu Kush?
What keeps the hopes of its people alive?

O Gandhari!* Take off your blindfold
and shield your children with your miraculous power.

O, Buddhas of the land! Share the secrets of peace and *Nirvana*.
My hopes are shattered like your statues—blown with dynamite.

Unlike you, I'm afraid of Angulimaal,** who vows my fingers,
for I want to read and write, sing and dance.

I can no longer touch my *Oud* or weave a dream whirling the cosmos.
But the valley of Bamyan remains silent. Its cliffs stare blankly

like empty tombs robbed by the raiders,
where Buddhas stood once, tall and humble.

In the distance, a passing wind roars,
and the mountains reverb the *mantra*—

'Gaathe, Gaathe, Paragathe, Parasamgathe, Bodhi, Svaha!'
'Gone, gone, gone, everything is gone, landed to another shore!'***

Gandhari—The queen of Gandhara, in ancient India, was known for her miraculous power to protect one with the light of her eyes. Gandhara is now a part of Afghanistan and Pakistan.

**Angulimal—A bandit who wore garlands of fingers of his victims later became the Buddha's disciple and transformed into a saint.*

***Gathe, Gathe, Paragathe, Parasamgathe, Bodhi, Svaha' is the end mantra of the "Heart Sutra," the core of Buddhism.*

The Daughters of the Hindu Kush

A woman receives justice in an open court
delivered by the guardians of Gods word?
Her sin asks for every piece of stone hauled from

the mountains of the Hindu Kush— gateway to my home,
graveyards of my ancestors laid barren and cold,
cloisters of the legends never told.

We no longer want to talk about Afghanistan.
We are out. We are done with saving Sakineh and Malala,
bringing back our girls. We make conscious choices.

A crowd sits in a circle and watches justice being delivered.
There are many circles outside the circle invisible to our eyes.
She cannot escape. Her lover is not present in the open court.

Wasn't he supposed to receive justice too? For God's sake,
hear her say the words never added to our dictionaries.
Hush! Hush! Hush! Do not fuss!

I'm not sure if there would be a Congressional hearing for such cases
in my country. The photographer filming the court proceedings,
would he win a Pulitzer? Or *lose his hands if seen?*

Hush! Hush! Hush! Don't be obscene!
Keep your eyes closed if you can't watch.
The storms shall pass. The storms shall pass!

But they keep returning. Fear runs through my body.
The pain of the woman being flogged is familiar to my skin.
Our forebears were kins, dragged in chains,

centuries went in vain, serving the men carrying—
swords, sabers, and spears. Naked and cold,
they were auctioned and sold in Ghazna and Khorāsān,

Cairo, Basra, and beyond. Lashes rained on the bodies refusing to kneel
and sail off to distant lands. The lightning swords shattered their bones,
scorched their spirits; their saviors were gone, morphed into mounds of skulls.

Their homes and villages were destroyed. Carved in gold,
silver and stone, their idols disappeared, and I wonder—
will this woman's face appear on the cover of the *New York Times*,

in the headlines of *The Washington Post* and *Al Jazeera*?
Jeff Bezos, did you get a 360-degree view of this woman's body
while cruising in space?

Twitter bird, say a few words when you're over your priorities,
fly to her land to save humanity. Facebook, allow some space for
women without faces, disappeared without a trace in time.

The lashes piling on her body are peeling her skin bit by bit,
cleansing her sin? I do not understand a word of my kin,
I have forgotten the language of my people, our prayers.

It has been centuries, I haven't uttered a word.
I must void my myths now and forever.
Dipped in the red ink—seeping through my veins,

my fingers must write my accounts, and etch them on my tombstones
in every corner of the earth. My pain must be worth...
Dear God, do you know, when you send me a man to love,

ask me to carry him in my womb, give him birth, and strike me down,
I dig my nails into the ground and the earth tremors?
Yet, I do not hold you responsible for my sufferings.

My love, tell me for once, that you loved me.
Mother, hold my hand. I taste my blood in my mouth.
Cover me, I have wet my undergarments.

Angels, take my baby to heaven,
bury her safe in the clouds,
I'm losing her, bleeding from the bottom.

Grandma, bring the scissors, cut the umbilical cord
and sing me a song they can't hear.
I want to sleep, now.

Father, do you see, I am breaking like a seed?
My lungs have split, and my voice is escaping my vocal cords.
I'm not dying. I am being born into freedom.

The Great Departure

I saw a white horse in my dream and wondered,
if it was for *Siddhartha* to escape on
the night of yet another *Mahabhinishkraman?**

Or else, the horse was mine and had returned to me
to perform my own *Ashwamedha Yajna,***
as my ancestors once did?

The horse circles, and I wonder,
there is no world I wish to conquer,
but my army marches forward.

Those who wish to challenge my sovereignty
must stop the horse and battle with me.
But no one approaches.

I'm an empress now and must sacrifice my own horse,
for my victory is not to be challenged by anyone!
But I tremble instead and lay down my sword.

I hold the reins and soar, not knowing
that the horse is now challenged by
the empress herself.

The army follows.
My crown is seized.
The battle is over.

My prisoner is free at last.

Mahabhinishkraman*—Buddha's great renunciation of his family and kingdom and going forth in search of knowledge to end suffering.

Ashwamedha Yajna**—A horse sacrifice ritual performed by Kshatriya rulers to establish their imperial sovereignty during the Vedic era in India.

Inheritance isn't a Matter of Choice

The most humbling lessons of life
are learned instinctively.

We discover them while listening to
the murmurs of our hearts and the sounds of
ancient streams running through our blood vessels.

We find them in the encryption
and the grand design of our DNA.

Every cell of our body carries
the memories of our ancestors,
their torments and fears,

hopes and healings, songs and prayers,
handed down to us with the gift of life.

We inherit the dreams aborted from
the eyes of our forefathers and mothers.
Inheritance isn't a matter of choice.

We look into the eyes of the storms
and bear the torch, our forebears couldn't carry.

The most profound lessons of life remain obscure,
beyond the concept of time.
They appear in our dreams,

breakout in the beads of sweat in our nightmares,
inviting us to discover all that is hidden in us,
all that is safe in water, clouds, and space,

lying in ruins on earth,
waiting to be decoded.

The Wisdom of My Ancestors

> *"Beyond the blue horizon, where our ancestors*
> *Appear bearing gifts..."* —Joy Harjo *(Beyond Sunrise)*

Our ancestors appear beyond the horizon
offering wisdom and a reminder that the only thing
permanent in the world is impermanence.

All shapes and forms dismantle. Each shade and color fades.
Every sound fizzles, and every touch is meant to be void.

I do not know where I have come from, and where I will go,
the day I'm devoid of touch, color, sound and form that identify me.

The only thing I know is that I come and go.
Someday, I'll rise beyond the horizon
to tell this story to my children, continuing my journey.

Birds are Our Ancestors

Every morning I harvest
the early rays of the sun,
gather them in the blue basket of the sky,
and feed crows and sparrows.

Birds are our ancestors.
I pass this wisdom handed down to me
by my forebears
to every passerby.

Birds recognize me.
They come flying when I call,
echoing the sky with
their enchanting sounds.

And I wonder—
the day I'm gone and
return to the earth on my wings,
who will recognize me?

The Caged Bird

The bird is the path.
The bird is the destination.
The bird is the focus.
The bird is the distraction.

Only the bird in the cage knows
the secrets of emancipation.

The Bridge

With the yarn of my invisible breaths
I weave a suspension bridge
in the lap of the cosmos
and cross over it.

I have built numerous bridges
like the one I travel on
since time unknown, and
severed them when I've gone.

Searching forever, my home,
I arrive with my in-breath,
with my out-breath, I leave,
with a promise to return.

When Everything Becomes a Calling

There is a time to speak
There is time not to speak.
There is a time to sleep.
There is a time not to sleep.

I sleep when the world is awake.
I'm awake when the world is in slumber.
I'm not a *Yogi,* just an ordinary poet,
working all day and writing at night.

When the sky sets up a stage for
the night and dawn to duet before their parting
and plays an orchestra for the choirs of birds
singing on distant boughs, I go to bed.

Nothing is determined by me.
Who does this so? I do not know.
Or maybe I do, without knowing,
the secrets are hidden within me.

Let the Water Sit All Night

Let the water sit all night, drink it in the morning.

The earthenware brought from the potter's place
filled with hand-pumped water extracted from the well
were left in the courtyard all night. The water soaked—

the shimmer of the stars and the hum of the easterly winds,
spreading the aroma of the earth, near and far. Be patient!
The moon floated in the vessel and whispered, when I lifted the lid.

The earthenware, tall and round, spun on the potter's wheel,
were pieces of art. The wind, the waiting, and watching,
the water refining in the stillness was science.

What I drank from my cup that day was knowledge.

The impurities settle when the water is still.
The breathing vessels keep the water chilled.
Back then, there were no fridges and filters at home.

The mind is nothing but tainted water in our body of clay,
spun on the wheel of the unknown.
Be still, breathe like earthenware, and cool off.

The vessels appear in my memories
like Buddhas sitting in the lotus pose,
on a moonlit night, under the Summer sky,

bearing the secrets of Nirvana.

Tripitaka

In three baskets, there were meals
enough to serve everyone on the planet.

In three baskets, there were offerings
for the past, present, and future.

From the three baskets they ate
not to be hungry again in lifetimes.

From the three baskets, they learned
how to cook and serve the universe.

In the three baskets, they saw
the sun, moon and stars dwelling.

In the three baskets, they discovered
the mountains, rivers, and green fields.

In the three baskets, the rain poured
incessantly, for everyone thirsty on earth.

In the three baskets, they found
the recipe of *Nirvana*, written and unwritten.

*Tripitaka (the three bamboo baskets) is the collected discourses of the Buddha, written in the Pali language.

Dhaknesar

My grandmother would make a dessert
with fragrant white rice thinly ground on stone,
pouring the batter slowly, in batches,
in sizzling earthenware, covered with a lid.

She would bake the cakes slowly,
on woodfire, and dip them gently in the syrup
made of milk, cardamom, and raw brown sugar,
before serving it warm in ceramic bowls.

Grandma had brought the recipe from
her village in Bhojpur. *Dhaknesar!*
What a funny name for dessert! Us children often giggled.
My aunts called the dish *Gujguji* instead.

No one knew what *Dhaknesar* was until Grandma made it.
She taught the recipe to everyone, and we knew—
It was round, white, and shiny, like the moon.
It was sweet, spongy, light, and airy like a cloud,

thickened with the taste of the earth,
scented with the fragrance of the woodfire.
You won't find this dessert in the City of Angels.
No one knows about this dish in America.

My children think it's a made-up dish. But it isn't.
Someday, I want to make *Dhaknesar* for my family
in the USA. Someday, I want to own a grinding stone
and a woodfire stove like Grandma and cook—

under the tent of the sky in my courtyard. Someday,
I would like to invite the entire world to taste this dessert,
which carries the aroma of the fire and earth
traveling from the lands of my ancestors.

*Dhaknesar is a Bhojpuri dessert from the state of Bihar in India.

Roots

My mother no longer wants to live where
she lived all her years. She wants to go elsewhere.
Where there is no suffering and fear of death.

But I had returned, only to inherit her fears,
and the fear of having everything she never had
and knowing—there is no death for a life never lived.

But now standing alone, under the blistering sun,
where my mother stood once, like an evergreen tree,
I hope that someday my mother shall return with the rain.

Another Shore

You do not realize it until the day
they have journeyed to another shore,
that they were the soles of your shoes
and the skin shielding your bones
from fire and frost. Mother, I'm cold.
Father, my feet are sore with blisters.

America

This time, when I boarded the plane
to return to America, I felt a peace within.
A peace that had finally returned to me after years.

This time, I did not fly on the wings of imagination
or dreams. I flew on the wings of aluminum and steel
that would finally take me home, away from my home.

Would it make me a lesser daughter, sister, friend,
or patriot, if I were not able to see the land below,
rising from the ground up in the air,

with my eyes filled with tears, saltier than my Indian sea?
Would it be unfair to say I'm destined for
a safe island, still quivering in hope?

Among hundreds of faces sitting on the plane,
I could easily identify the face of America, and its smile
served to me like a warm blanket in my seat, for me to

peacefully fall asleep and migrate into my soul,
silently, no longer in search of a land of opportunity, but love,
that knows no boundaries of nations, my ultimate destination.

Invocation

I haven't spoken to the mother in months.
But I know she is there. She can't disappear.
She can't be imprisoned or killed. I wonder if she is sleeping.
"Jago Ma Jago!" Be awakened, Mother Goddess!

My mother is the daughter of the Himalayas.
On the occasion of *Mahalaya*, I cannot stop thinking about her
and all her relatives, like *Shiva* and *Parvati*, their little boy *Ganesha*,
their bull, and all others who live in Kashmir.

Shailputri, the daughter of the mountains, I hope you are doing well.
I hope you have the freedom to go anywhere you want.
I hope the mobile network is working in your area.
Do you have enough food and water in your cave?

I hope your trees are still bearing fruits
and your glaciers are kind to your rivers.
I hope your valley is still growing flowers
and the dark clouds are filled with rain.

Mother, have you talked to *Shiva* and *Parvati*,
peasants and boatmen, saints and *Pirs*, after
the abrogation of *370*? How are you taking it yourself?
I hope little *Ganesha* is not afraid of going to school.

I hope no one has thrown stones at you and your people
still love you. I hope no one has hassled and raped you
and the world is only lying. Brahmacharini,
the sacred one, you do not know,

the reporting of *The New York Times, B.B.C.,*
The Washington Post and *Al Jazeera* cause me to worry.
They write all is not well in Kashmir.
Although the Prime Minister says, *All is well.*

Mother, I do not know whom to believe,
my friends from the Left or the Right,
my friends from the East or the West.
To keep my hopes alive, I only watch Indian and Canadian news.

Chandraghante, you have helped Mission *Chandrayan.*
Can't you protect your own abode? Can't you bless your own land?
"Jago Ma Jago!" Be awakened, Mother Goddess!

The *Muezzin* is calling for prayers.

Mother, go to Srinagar to meet Abdullah and Mufti.
Go to Ladakh to reassure monks and nuns in *Gompas*.
In Jammu, visit the Pandits, void of hope,
still living in refugee camps in their homeland.

Kushmanda, the creator of the universe, create a new Kashmir.
Wash your wounds with five rivers. Call *Hanuman* to fetch *Sanjivani,*
revive the dead sleeping in graves, and soldiers bleeding
on the borders in snowstorms.

They are all your children, born from your eternal womb.
Sing them the songs of *Sufis* that you have fed them
through your breast milk. Bring out your *Santoor, Veena,* and *Rabab,*
your children are afraid of the sound of silence, guns, and explosions!

Skandamata, summon your brave son, *Skanda,*
chosen by the gods to lead
in the war against evil.
Bring victory to all your offspring.

Bring light to the eyes that can no longer see.
Bring joy to the hearts that cannot sing.
Bring your children home for celebrations.
It has been long, so long…

Katyayani, let your lion roar in the mountains
and tell the demons not to venture into your homeland!
Invite *Kalhana* and *Tarantha* to write a new chapter
in the history of Paradise on Earth. A history the world must envy.

Kalratri, the fierce one,
let all your ten hands work harder,
day and night, twenty-four-hours.
There is a lot to do in the valley.

Call Hazrat Makhdoom in Sopore, Sheikh Nur-ud-din in Kulgam,
call Hieun Tsang from China. Invite *Arhats, Bodhisattvas,
Shankaracharya* and *Kashyapa,* to give you a hand in draining
the blood from the ancient lake and regaining paradise.

Let your donkey carry the bags of apples and peaches,
herbs and almonds, medicines and *Pashmina,*
to deliver to the homes that cannot wait to open

their doors and windows to the sunlight.

Mahagauri, the fair one,
let the world envy your luminous beauty and wisdom,
that sparkles the water of *Dal Lake* and the cliffs of
your glorious mountains dipped in saffron.

The evil may return again to stain your splendor.
But do not let anyone touch you over.
Do not let them steal you from your horses,
grazing in orchards and violate you in your temple!

Siddhidatri, the bestower of all blessings,
someday, when peace returns to Kashmir,
invite *Habba Khatoon, Lal Ded, Shahid Ali,*
and all other poets of your land for a poetry reading in a *Shikara*.

And please, keep open for poets like *Huzaifa* and me.
I have earned an invitation from him to visit Kashmir,
after a long argument that I won with him.
Do not invite press and media without credentials,

but allow a visa to Jamil, across from L.O.C.
He likes poetry and wants to see Srinagar.
The Srinagar of Raja Gulab Singh, his King.
But please, do not tell him that—

there are no kings and queens in Kashmir anymore.
They all died in a *Raid* long ago, and
their subjects have been defeated in the game of
Check and Mate, we all have played along together.

---

*The Mother, addressed by different names, is the ten manifestations of Goddess Durga, also known as Vaishno Devi, who resides in the Himalayas, in the Union Territories of Jammu and Kashmir

Blood and Water

Simply a Witness

Storms in the desert roared,
as we prayed before the first bullet
came out of our triumphant guns.

The skin of the earth peeled and burned
as the pages of history turned.

I'm not here to decide
whether a war is just or unjust.
I'm Time, simply a witness.

The Last Soldier

The last soldier leaving
Hamid Karzai airport was carrying—

two thousand two hundred and eighteen coffins
on his shoulder.

Sunflower

I draw a sunflower in the sand and toss it up into the sky.

Grab it if you can, and hand it to that little Ukrainian boy
walking alone, in tears, toward the border of a foreign land.

The plastic bag he carries, has a message for the world.
The red diary he holds, has the offenses of history.

The burdens on his shoulders are ours.
He is tired—give him the flower.

He stops suddenly, refusing to walk
in the direction the world is going.

In his *halt* are the hopes for the future.

Ground Zero

Splitting the lungs of the sky
a shell drops like an hourglass of fire,
on the heart of Zaporizhzhia,
emptying itself to the last atom.

The hole left in the heart of the earth
fills with the cries of millions
fleeing their homes.
Every heart in a war is ground zero.

War: A One Way Street

Driving in my town,
I imagine sirens blaring, tanks rolling,
and guns pointing at people resisting.

I see no dove flying in the sky.
The olive trees are eradicated from
every corner of the earth.

I shiver in fear, like a leaf on an amputated branch.
My children are home, but I can't turn around.
War is a one-way street. We can only pull back.

The hospitals are filled with injured and burnt bodies.
The buildings and homes are engulfed in fire.
I have no weapon to fight. I may not return home tonight.

War is a phenomenon, the accumulation of our thoughts and actions.
What goes on in our minds, manifests in the world.

The idea of who we are is not limited to our narrow discretion.
I'm a person, and a nation, an ally, and an adversary.

I'm a woman raped and mutilated by my enemies,
and a limb hanging from the window of a building struck.

I'm a fallen soldier who died defending his country.
And my slayer does not know what he is fighting for.

I am bent like the little girl, pulled up by force on the last train
about to leave the station, bound to a foreign land.

I'm the agony of a father in exodus, without his sons and daughters.
I'm a sorrow, frozen in the eyes of a young girl who presses her palm

against the windowpane of a train, to touch the hands of the men
staying behind to fight for their country.

I'm the blood-crusted snow after a night of
heavy shelling on my falling city.

There is no glory in a war. Every home has a shrine.
A war cannot be defined. It can only be lived or imagined.

War and Flowers

The flowers did not go to the weddings and birthdays as planned,
the christenings of the newborns, or to profess love for valentines.
They did not sit at homes in vases. They refused to go
to the palaces of dictators and monarchs.

They did not go to the temples, churches and synagogues,
or offer themselves to God and Godmen.
They went to honor the coffins of the soldiers
and unmarked graves of the brave and innocents.

They traveled to the borders to welcome refugees
and sat on shrines to pray for peace.
And before they wilted in fire and snow,
the flowers scattered their seeds to regrow.

Everyone takes a new role in a war.

My Post Office Without a Country

—After Agha Shahid Ali

Every so often, nations fall from the world map,
as leaves and flowers fall from a tree hit by a thunderstorm.

My poetry book cannot travel to the Holy Land.

Palestine isn't in the database of the United States Postal Office.
I verify the address given to me by Mohammad.

How could a country disappear into space?

People standing in the queue look at my face.
The clerk turns the screen toward me and scrolls down.

The State of Palestine wasn't found.

My package was returned. And as I turned, I saw someone smiling at me.
Palestine exists in the twinkles of her eyes.

It exists because Mohammad lives there. He tells us the stories of his land.
It exists because Yaseer Arafat came to my homeland in a *Keffiyeh*.
It exists because I hear Palestine sing in *Tarana* of Rim Banna.
It exists because it burns in the eyes of Ahed Tamimi.
It exists because it lives in the hearts of five million *Philistines*.

I'll exit the line, but tell me first, how Palestine went missing?
I ask *Handala*. I ask my friend Mohammad in Ramallah,

Sartawi in Jordan and Ronni in Galilee.
I ask Shahid Ali of *The Country Without a Post Office*.

I ask this question to myself as I write—
My Post Office Without a Country.

Love that Cannot Live Long Enough

Not long ago
I was Kosovo,

then became Baghdad
by the Tigris.

Then I turned into Syria
and Ukraine,

crippled and bled to death.
Only to wake up again,

without any eyes or limbs,
without any heart or soul.

And today, I'm Gaza,
covered in ashes,

shooting rockets,
siphoning missiles and bullets.

You can call me hatred
or hope that cannot die.

Or love that cannot live
long enough.

Language

I wonder about the first language of the child
survived in a hospital hit by a rocket.

His mother cannot speak anymore.

The Temples of Knowledge

—A tribute to all libraries and archives in the world destroyed by humans

The war has destroyed the largest bookstore in Gaza.
A handful of people are protesting at an intersection.
No one is taking notice, except for those

who are watching live T.V.
Some vehicles honk their support.
The storekeeper grieves, and I grieve along.

History repeats itself more often than we realize. I mourn for Gaza.
Moreover, for the Mouseion of Alexandria, the archives of
Antioch, Isfahan, Ghazna, Nishapur, Cambodia, Cairo, and Syria.

I rue for the libraries of Beirut, Baghdad, Mosul, and Mali,
Washington, Warsaw, Mandalay, Madrid, and more.
Is anyone keeping score?

More so, I mourn for Nalanda, burning in its ruins forever.
The temple of knowledge destroyed...
Who had arrived? Who had arrived?

Who had arrived to conquer the unconquered,
trampling the footsteps of the Buddha
under the hooves of his horses?

The university was torched not once, but twice, not twice,
but thrice. Teachers and students captured and burnt alive...
Monks executed... The meanings of texts converted...

Who had arrived? Who had arrived,
flaying the skin of the sky
with his sword, eclipsing the sun

shining on the temples of knowledge
in Nalanda, Taxila, Jagaddala,
Odantapuri and Vikramshila?

The tents were pitched with the leather of the nights
on the sacred grounds of *Arhats* and *Bodhisattvas,*
the lands of my ancestors, the land of my birth.

The fire gnawed at the textbooks and scriptures for months.
The first university on earth burned and burned.
It continues to burn to this day in its ruins and repines

for every shrine of knowledge on earth.
Close your eyes to see all you cannot see with your eyes open,
and open your heart to let go of the pain.

When I grieve for Gaza, I grieve for
all the athenaeums destroyed in the world,
every archive lost in space.

When I grieve for Nalanda,
I grieve alone and wonder why.
The world didn't expect me to survive.

The Peacebroker

Baying for blood, more blood,
nurtured by blood I was born
and have become mightier ever since.

I wonder, just as you do—is it too late?
Or is it never too late to return
to the sanctuary of peace?

No one knows the blood trade better than I do.
I peruse every market on the globe,
selecting only the finest bargains.

I guard my secrets, divulging to none.
I can pay any price, as long as
the offer is enticing.

And as the sky ignites like a fired grill and smoke rises,
I recline in my seat, contemplating the cut
I yearn to have it on my dinner plate.

The Best Kept Secret

When I first learned the phrase *"dirt poor,"*
I regarded it as just another expression
to call someone impoverished.

Much later, I realized—its meaning had more to it,
beyond the imaginations of many of us
who studied humanities in elite schools.

I discovered the true definition of the term
while eating my toast at home at my dining table,
in the world's most affluent country,

watching T.V., planning my next meal, as
I watched a mother make mud cakes for her family,
in a remote village in Africa.

She molded the mud little by little with water
like my mother kneaded the flour dough
to make breakfast for our family every morning.

Her children eating the cake, had rainbows in their eyes
without rain. Is this what being dirt poor means?
All of a sudden I'm enlightened!

These children, perhaps, will never go to school.
They will never taste a glass of freshly pressed orange juice or
eat a boiled egg at their breakfast. There is no water in their village.

They walk miles, to fetch drinking water home every day.
Eating my toast treated with imported butter,
I wondered about the taste of a mud cake,

how it is baked to perfection in the sun,
what elements of earth go into making a perfect mud cake,
what aroma releases when it melts in the mouth.

The recipe for a mud cake is nowhere to be found.
It's a delicacy, but no chef is trained to make mud cakes
in our exclusive culinary schools.

No restaurant on the globe has it on its menu.
The mud cake recipe is the best-kept secret on earth,
under lock and key of the nations united and defeated.

Alan Kurdi

In his veins, the blood of his ancestors,
in his fragile breath, the storms of his nation.

In his lungs, the rough water of a sea
he could not cross.

He shed tears of blood before closing his eyes.
The ocean swallowed his mother and brother.

Beyond the reach of his small arms were
our promised land and safe havens.

He was washed ashore, like a doll, lifeless,
face down, as if, kneeling in prayers.

His name was Alan Kurdi.
He was three.

Jamila of Idlib

Happiness isn't always what we wish for.
Sometimes, it is the absence of
what we do not wish for ourselves.

It has been seven years since
Jamila has left her home and
the man she was married to.

She wonders if he ever made it to
the European shore? Did he ever
look for her and their children?

He wasn't Love. He was a monster.
Her scars are still fresh on her mind.
She sighs under the heap of torment.

She no longer waits for his return.
She looks into the eyes of her children and smiles.
Jamila is a happy refugee in Jordan.

Line of Control

Last night, I was face to face
with my enemy.
No dagger was drawn.

The world was fast asleep
as we stitched
each other's wounds.

Centuries torn into pieces
descended from the moon
to bind up our wounds.

We washed our hands and faces
in the river *Sapphire* and kissed the earth.
We didn't pray. We recited poetry.

Dreamers

They continue to dream
on sleepless nights,
clenching stars in their fists
somewhere in the middle of nowhere,
across a fence, across the border,
across a river and ocean.

The sun no longer rises in the east
and sets in the west.
The earth moves backward and trips over.
The world is only upside down,
when we think—
we are atop the sky.

Displaced

I am a seed,
the earth requires
no clearance for me to grow.

I am a bird
the sky sets
no limits for me to fly.

But one day
they came to uproot us,
clip our wings, and bury us,

neither dead nor alive
beneath our broken feathers.

The Painted Ladies of Baja

The Painted Ladies of Baja have arrived,
in their colorful skirts and silken scarves.

The walls and fences of my country are
bowing to their beauty

and letting them cross the border,
without a visa or passport, without any court order.

Our land has been invaded, but
no one is worried, except for our politicians.

Our soldiers have gone on strike,
no one is taking any orders.

No gun is ready to point and shoot,
no missile is willing to boot and launch

and they are soaring above the beaches and canyons,
highways and freeways, stopping traffic.

A Painted Lady in my backyard—poses for a picture,
and asks me—*Where have You come from?*

The Dance of the Century

At the Sound of Tsuzumi

Behind the masks are eyebrows,
cheekbones and jawlines.
The faces have disappeared.

The one who has stolen all faces has no face.
Or maybe it does, 6.83 million and counting.
Stretched up to the horizon in the arena—

it appears on the stage like a Kabuki performer
and disappears with a generation
stuffed in its Kimono.

It is the dance of the century.
The sky is a drum
beating all night.

We slip on the mask of the moon
and dance alone and together.
We learn the steps unlearned.

At the curious sounds of *Tsuzumi*
we rise, breathing deeply—
and breathless, we fall.

O Captain!

    —*After Walt Whitman*

You cannot blame it all on June gloom,
sitting in your living room, surfing channels,
watching plague, politics, and war.

I turn the TV off and read Whitman—
"*O Captain! my Captain!...*"
"*O the bleeding drops of red...*"

I can't wait for the sun to arrive in the eastern hemisphere.
The night sails like a mammoth ship in dark rivers, scooping the dead.
My father, mother, sister, and brother are ailing. Friends have left too soon.

Hark! I hear the faint moaning of the cities shackled from afar.
The buildings hang from the sky lifeless, their tongues out the windows.
The doors are closed, but oxygen has escaped.

There aren't enough wood and shrouds left in the market.
Like doctors, nurses and essential staff, the forests working
around the clock are making oxygen, coffins, and kindling wood for cremation.

The animals on the graves appear orphaned. Their masters have left.
The banyan trees stand humble in the country carrying clay pots
hanging from their necks, like the *Bhistis** offering water—

to the thirsty souls wandering in the state of *Bardo.***
Shiva*** roams with his third eye open
in villages and towns and charnel grounds,

emitting fire from the center of his brows,
lighting pyres of those abandoned on river beds,
drinking toxins—flowing in the water to purify the rivers.

Covered in ashes as the embers fly,
he contains the spread. He does not exhale.
He is blue, turning darker blue.

The Himalayas melt in grief.
The Ganges widens her shores.
There are more pyres on the ground tonight than stars *lit* in the sky.

The truth sounds like a lie. But it isn't.
There aren't enough beds and oxygen in the hospitals.
There aren't enough vaccines and medical supplies.

Who is accountable? Who is accountable?
Who is accountable? I beg for help—
help the helpless!

Friends, who couldn't come forward have promised,
they will forward my plea to the rich *NRIs*.****
A slap, right in my face!

For the first time, I'm angry
for not being rich enough like Gates,
to help my country breathe with one fat check.

Why do I worry? Thirty-three million gods will take care of everything.
Why do I bother? 1.36 billion people will manage their country.
O sister, you will be okay. O Mother, try to sleep now.

I shall breathe for you with my lungs expanded to the continents.
Hope isn't a luxury. It is a necessity.
I invite the *Bell****** and sit in silence.

I write an alphabet on a piece of paper and repeat,
until it burns a hole in my heart.
O for Oxygen, O for Oxygen, O for Oxygen.

"O Captain! my Captain! rise up and hear the bells."

This poem was composed in the wake of the deadly second wave of COVID-19

*Bhistis—*Traditional water bearers from a Tribe in India and Pakistan.*
**Bardo—*A transitional state between death and rebirth.*
***Shiva—*A Hindu deity of Annihilation and Purification.*
****NRIs—*Non-Resident Indians.*
*****Bell—*Meditation Bell.*

Is Anyone Listening?

She has lost her mind. It's impossible to care for her.
A WhatsApp message notifies in the middle of the night.
I promise not to talk about the messenger.

They are considering a mental asylum or a senior home.
They are waiting for her lab results and the doctor's note.
She no longer has a say.

She can't remember her whereabouts, sits half-naked
all day. She can no longer button her blouse,
can't clean herself. She is a mess.

She can't stand unsupported, unable to walk even a little distance.
She refuses her cane and hopes. She is convinced
it's time for her to go now.

Her hands—like branches of desiccating tree
birds have abandoned. Her hollow bones sing all night
the lullaby her mother sang to her. But she cannot sleep.

She can't remember the days of the week,
the number of years she has lived. Do you?
Do the math, you brainiac!

Add her age with the ages of all her children and grandchildren.
She lives in their flesh, blood, and bone marrow. Let's not forget,
she is just living on the plane where we yet have to arrive.

She can't keep track of time, doesn't know if it's day or night,
and keeps calling. *Cut the crap! Send her to a madhouse!*
Shut out the noises she makes—just a bit of advice.

It's a lockdown, and she wants to go elsewhere.
Where to she doesn't know. Millions have lost their jobs,
and she has lost her mind! Millions have died, but she is still living.

It's easier said than done.
You privileged ones, sitting afar,
you are only eligible to foot her bills and be entertained.

People are dying of hunger, and she is wasteful,
smears her food all over her body and face, worse than a child.
She soiled the elevator the other day. How embarrassing!

She needs a diaper change every two hours.
Go away, you perfect mess! Stop knocking!
People are working from home, don't you know?

They have bills to pay, family to care for.
But she keeps coming and coming,
knocking and knocking,

until a door opens, and she feels a blow on her face,
punch after punch on her forehead, until she collapses,
choking on her children's names, and goes silent.

The Poet is Gone

The poet is gone. The poet is gone, leaving a chest behind.

In the chest, there are a thousand letters to a dictator,
hundreds to his followers and one to himself about his dream of
becoming a singer and someday living on farmland.

His being as a poet was accidental.
The burden of earning bread and butter
had dragged him to the city from his mountain abode.

From the capital's streets to the bulletin room,
he covered every piece of news and more.
He was worried about pollution and the virus that could kill

the masses of his nation in droves. In his worries,
he forgot all about his dreams. And as he sipped his last drink
and made one last ring of smoke sitting at his writing table,

he realized it was too late. His organs gave up.
His lungs collapsed. Tied in a hospital bed all alone,
he wanted to sing but couldn't. He tried to write a note but failed.

His poems were timbers from mountains, fired up with his spirit.
The flame he ignited lit many candles and consumed his dreams.
The poet is gone. The poet is gone, leaving a legend behind.

Pandemic

My neighbor is a frontline worker.
She is the breadwinner in her family.
No one knows her real name. We call her Kimmy.

She dresses up like a doctor.
But she isn't a doctor. She is just afraid of
bringing the virus home and passing it on to her children.

Her children are grown up, but they aren't kind.
Today, they left home to live elsewhere.
They are going to be safer now, Kimmy explains.

She has the entire house by herself now,
fridge stocked with food, milk, water bottles,
and thirty rolls of toilet paper to survive the Pandemic.

Kimmy is Vietnamese, often mistaken for being Chinese.
She laughs and tells me in the parking lot—
"It isn't a good time to be Asian." But she isn't fazed.

She rolls up her sleeves and drives away.
She takes people home from hospitals.
She reads their faces in the rearview mirror and asks—

"How is your day going?"
They try to smile behind their masks.
Thanks to Corona for less traffic and smog!

Before going to bed, Kimmy calls her parents in Vietnam.
They say—*they are doing good in their country,*
And Kimmy tells them—*she's doing good in America.*

ER

My case wasn't serious, so
I waited in the lobby of the ER
for my turn.

Patients needed to have patience.
Except those who showed severe symptoms
like fever, nausea, and fits.

But I didn't vomit. My temperature remained stable.
And I was able to hold the ground,
like a tree standing in a storm.

I did not show any cuts or bruises.
I did not bleed or collapse,
like some others did…

and were rushed into rooms
where the doctors were ready to diagnose
and treat them immediately.

I just had some internal injuries no one knew.
I bled inside. I died in front of everyone,
without anyone noticing me.

Additional Acknowledgments

I would like to express my deepest gratitude to Candice Louisa Daquin and Melissa Studdard for their invaluable contributions in shaping *Trespassing My Ancestral Lands*. Their insights, feedback, suggestions, and copy editing have greatly enhanced the overall impact of the book.

My heartfelt thanks to Candice Louisa Daquin for penning the foreword of *Trespassing My Ancestral Lands*. Candice, you've captured the very soul of the book with eloquence and depth, surpassing all my expectations. I am truly grateful to you.

I would also like to extend my deepest appreciation to Cynthia Atkins, Jennifer Reeser, Beau Beausoleil, Anita Nahal, and Octavio Quintanilla for dedicating their time to read the manuscript of *Trespassing My Ancestral Lands* and providing their insightful blurbs. Your profound understanding of my book has left me in awe.

To my family and loved ones, I am forever grateful for your unwavering encouragement and inspiration throughout my creative journey. Shashwat, Vishwa, and Nirvan, your faith in me and my work have been a constant source of motivation to bring this book to fruition.

Furthermore, I want to express my sincere thanks to Finishing Line Press for providing me with the opportunity to publish *Trespassing My Ancestral Lands*. Your belief in my work and support are deeply appreciated.

Last but not least, I want to thank my readers. Your engagement with my words is my ultimate reward. Thank you, from the bottom of my heart, for being a part of this incredible journey.

With profound appreciation,

Kalpna Singh-Chitnis

Kalpna Singh-Chitnis is an Indian-American poet, writer, filmmaker, and author of six poetry collections. Her works have appeared in notable journals such as *World Literature Today, Columbia Journal, Tupelo Quarterly, Cold Mountain Review, Indian Literature, Vsesvit, Silk Routes* (IWP) at The University of Iowa, and Stanford University's *Life in Quarantine*. Kalpna Singh-Chitnis has been referenced in renowned publications such as the *New York Times* and *Huffington Post*, and featured in *The Telegraph, OC Register, Los Angeles Times, Daily Pilot,* and others. She has made appearances on major broadcasting platforms like ABC Channel 7, Voice of America, Fox News, India's National TV Network, Doordarshan, KPFK Radio, and various additional television and radio networks. Her poetry has been translated into twenty languages and has been included in college and university curricula in India and in the UK.

Her bilingual poetry collection *Love Letters to Ukraine from Uyava*, translated into Ukrainian by Volodymyr Tymchuk, a poet and Lieutenant Colonel of The Armed Forces of Ukraine, was honored as a finalist in the 2023 "International Book Awards" presented by American Book Fest. Additionally, *Sunflowers: Ukrainian Poetry on War Resistance, Hope, and Peace*, an anthology curated and edited by her was named a finalist in the 2023 "National Indie Excellence Awards."

Kalpna's poetry has received praise from eminent writers, such as Nobel Prize in Literature nominee Dr. Wazir Agha, Vaptsarov Award and Ordre des Arts et des Lettres recipient Amrita Pritam, and poet and Academy Award-winning lyricist and filmmaker Gulzar. She has read at the International Literature Festival Berlin (ilb), Sahitya Akademi, India's highest academy of letters, AWP Conferences, *Poets & Writers*, and other venues internationally.

As a filmmaker, she is known for her feature film *Goodbye My Friend*, short film *Girl With An Accent* and her environmental film *The Tree*, based on her work of poetry. Her films have garnered multiple awards at international film festivals, including the "Silver Award" for her short film *Girl With An Accent* and the "Best Experimental Short Film Award" at the North Dakota Environmental Rights Film Festival.

She has been nominated for a pushcart prize, and her awards and honors include the 2017 "Naji Naaman Literary Prize for Creativity," the "Bihar Rajbhasha Parishad Award," given by the government of Bihar, India, "Bihar Shri," and the "Rajiv Gandhi Global Excellence Award." Poems from her award-winning book *Bare Soul* and her poetry film *River of Songs,* included in the *Nova Collection* and the *Polaris Collection* archived in the Lunar Codex time capsule, landed on the moon with Odysseus, in a joint mission of NASA, SpaceX, and Intuitive Machines in 2024. A former lecturer of Political Science and Editor-in-Chief of *Life and Legends,* she works as an independent filmmaker in Hollywood and serves as an Advocacy Member at the United Nations Association of the USA.

Website: www.kalpnasinghchitnis.com

www.ingramcontent.com/pod-product-compliance
Lightning Source LLC
Chambersburg PA
CBHW020337170426
43200CB00006B/415